The Typists Play Monopoly

The Typists Play Monopoly

Poems by

Kathleen McClung

Kelsay Books

Cover: Clara Peeters, *Vanitas Self-Portrait*, c. 1610
    (Painting in the public domain)

Author photo: Hilary Buffum

ISBN: 978-1-947465-60-2

Kelsay Books
White Violet Press
www.kelsaybooks.com

for Tom

Acknowledgments

Many thanks to the editors of the publications in which these poems appeared, sometimes in a slightly different version.

Atlanta Review: "Anticipators"
California Quarterly: "At the Marin Art Festival"
Caesura: "Velocity"
Chronicles of Eve: "Clara Peeters, *Vanitas Self-Portrait*, c. 1610"
CSPS Poetry Letter: "Perfect Game"
Ekphrasis: "Behind the White Bird"
Forgotten Women: A Tribute in Poetry: "Laura Knight, *Self-Portrait*, 1913," and "Alice Neel, *Nude Self-Portrait*, 1980"
Marin Poetry Center Anthology: "For the Man at Macy's Lurking in Swimwear," and "Nashville Labyrinth"
Mezzo Cammin: "Renter Sonnet: A Leased Crown," "Clutter Song," "Many Visitors Have Been Gored," and "Ticket Stub"
Noyo River Review: "Gilbert and Ed Washing the Wheelchairs, Telegraph Avenue Coin-Op"
Peacock Journal: "A Broken World: Cento for Jane Clarke"
PoetryMagazine.com: "Anticipators," "For the Man at Macy's Lurking in Swimwear," and "Velocity"
Poets 11 2010: "Why We Have Windows"
Poets 11 2014: "Anticipators," "Bridgework: A Span of Sonnets"
Postcard Poems and Prose: "Phone Call in a New Century: Cento for Lynne Barnes"
Sin Fronteras: "Breaking Bad Sonnet"
Stirring: A Literary Collection: "The Traffic Reporter's Retirement Speech"
The Gathering 13: "Perfect Game"
Tilt-a-Whirl: "Vacancies"
Unsplendid: "Sestina in Late June," "Lighter Than Her Lace: A Crown of Borrowed Self-Portraits"

Verseweavers: "My Mother's Cold War"
West Trestle Review: "Souvenir Corkscrew"
WinningWriters.com: "Lighter Than Her Lace: A Crown of Borrowed Self-Portraits"
Writing in a Woman's Voice: "Nashville Labyrinth," and "Perfect Game"
Zoomorphic: "The Elder"

These poems were honored:

"Considering Chess, Tomales Bay:" First prize in the Legacy category of the 2015 Ina Coolbrith Circle Poetry Contest and first prize in the Jim Stone Memorial category of the Springfield Writers' Guild 2015 Contest. "The Typists Play Monopoly:" Salem College 2012 Rita Dove Poetry Award, first prize in the Cultural Center of Cape Cod 2012 national poetry competition, and first prize in the 2014 Dancing Poetry Contest. "May the Road Rise Up:" 2016 Louise Bogan prize from the Massachusetts State Poetry Society. "Ribs:" First prize in the Mini category of the Bay Area Poets Coalition Maggi H. Meyer Memorial Contest 34. "Gilbert and Ed Washing the Wheelchairs, Telegraph Avenue Coin-Op:" First prize in the Midi category of the BAPC Maggi H. Meyer Memorial Contest 35. "The Elder:" First prize in the formal poetry category of the Illinois State Poetry Society 2014 Contest. "Laura Knight, *Self-Portrait*, 1913:" First prize in the category of persona poem in Green River Writers 2014 Contest. "Lighter Than Her Lace: A Crown of Borrowed Self-Portraits:" Finalist for the 2016 Margaret Reid Poetry Prize. The following poems also appeared in the chapbook, *Almost the Rowboat*, published by Finishing Line Press: "Sestina in Late June," "The Typists Play Monopoly," and "Why We Have Windows."

Many people supported, nudged and nourished me in the making of this book. Thank you to Karen Kelsay and Sarah Stark for their grace and expertise. Bouquets to poets Kim Bridgford, Holly J. Hughes, and Indigo Moor: You are luminous. I am so fortunate to have inspiring colleagues at Skyline College and The Writing Salon: Mary Gutiérrez, Marijane Datson, Katharine Harer, Rob Williams, Kathleen Azevedo Feinblum, Jim Bowsher, Kevin Chak, Ben Jackson, Alison Luterman, Julie Bruck, Lori Ostlund. Members of writing groups on both sides of the bay keep deepening my work: Grace Marie Grafton, Tobey Hiller, Carol Dorf, Ramsay Bell Breslin, Catherine Freeling, Tobey Kaplan, Maw Shein Win, Heather Bourbeau, Lynne Barnes, Chris Cook. I treasure the vibrant Bay Area poetry community: Eileen Malone, Ellaraine Lockie, Robert Eastwood, Dawn McGuire, Connie Post, Casey FitzSimons, Diane Lee Moomey, Fred Dodsworth, Andrena Zawinski, and all who live and write here. My teachers and students over the years—way too many to name!—bring me joy and hope, and so do my beloved friends Chris Herlinger, Jennifer Moore Ballentine, Robin Severns, Nancy Buffum, Joe Dellert, Kathy Rice-Trumble, Val Habegger, Lisa Carlson, Ellen Woods, Lyzette Wanzer, Li Miao Lovett. I've had fruitful dialogue with Mary J. Ewert for over twenty years; many, many thanks. I am endlessly grateful to my parents, grandparents, sister Elizabeth, step-mom, step-sisters, nieces, nephews, uncles and aunts for their love and encouragement. And to my partner Tom McAninley: Thank you, Sweetie, for love, laughter, rope-a-dope with Burster, and chocolate.

Contents

III. Expiration Dates

IV. Lighter Than Her Lace: A Crown of Borrowed Self-Portraits

I. Lullaby in Reverse

My Mother's Cold War

You changed the channels on the black-and-white,
but talk of missiles did not end. Grim men
with maps of Cuba, Florida, the Keys
intoned all day and magnified despair. A stroke
had palsied Grandpa Mark the year before—
his walk a shuffle, and baseball chatter his words:

Watch 'im now. Keep your eye on 'im. Eight words
were all I ever heard him say for years, his white
hair neatly combed, his gray slacks pressed, and four
quick dabs, Old Spice, on cheeks and neck. Old men
moved slow, I knew back then, but most made sense. His stroke,
a mystery to me, a lock whose keys

got lost before my birth—that is, if keys
had ever truly fit. You said at two, I coined more words,
more sentences than he, and tender women stroked
my head at Lucky market—shoppers, white
and black, carts crammed with steaks, canned peas—women
like you, afraid, determined, stocking up before

the missiles launched, rose, arced and fell, before
grave captains onboard submarines turned keys
releasing bigger bombs, before all men
and women perished from the earth. Some words
did give you comfort, Mother, in your white
kitchen those autumn days. Perhaps the strokes

you made yourself with Bic ballpoint, small strokes,
secrets in Gregg shorthand. Or songs you'd heard before
by Nat King Cole. Did your head throb with the fridge's white-
noise hum? You said I chewed and praised my plastic keys:
red, jello, green, pink, blue. Perhaps my words
soothed you, lullaby in reverse, while men's

low voices murmured on TV, newsmen
cleancut, articulate, unscathed by stroke.
October, 1962—all of their words
intact and whole and horrible. Before
the crisis calmed, I wonder if you weighed your keys,
weighed idling the Ford behind closed white

garage door, drowsy passengers speaking few words—
man dulled by stroke, toddler in white nightgown.
But aisles of Lucky ladies knew our names, waited for us.

Considering Chess, Tomales Bay

A tethered boat—*King's Gambit*—beckons, and I draw
white-scalloped photograph from memory, slim piece
of family lore: My father at 16, crewcut
and freckled and *four-eyed*. He's poised to move.
He loves this game, this solid board, the way
each player calculates, deciding when

to sacrifice a pawn or rook, and when
to capture the queen. Exhibition match—a draw.
George Koltanowski shakes his hand, the way
grandmasters do, an ancient sign of peace
at battle's end, and afternoon fades, moves
to myth, no longer 1952 but

a tale enlarging over time: *He made the cut
from amateur to semi-pro! His win
would break a master's heart! Face-saving move,
Kolty conceding, we all know!* My father's draw,
a legend in our clan, a masterpiece
confirmed by blurry photograph the way

the Loch Ness Monster rises, sinks away.
I'm mixing metaphors. I ought to cut
aquatic beasts. And yet my bay retreat—this piece
of earth and water, pelicans and wind—
now lures and nets these drifting flecks and draws
them near: Old snapshot of a youth about to move

black bishop on a board. Old daughter, moved
by egrets, boats in slips, I labor now to weigh
which wisps of legacy to praise. How might I draw
conclusions, know which gifts of his to cut
or keep? I learn these rules at 7 when
the age of reason dawns: Recruit each piece

from velvet slot in cedar box. Revere the piece
commanding all, and pity those who only move
one square, the duds, expendable. And when
he murmurs, *Check*, blink back girls' tears, seek ways
to flee, forestall defeat. Choose brooding. Cut
through panic, grief. Choose vigilance. A childhood draws

to a close. Protect the king. Lose anyway.
Remove, return each piece to box, and dream of draws,
of gulls that cut across a bay, moored skiffs in wind.

Perfect Game

A quiet girl leaves on Saturdays before they wake,
delivers bottles of rum drizzle to the dump,
padlock combination leaking from her fingertips.

Alone on the mound, she pitches orange peels
to expectant gulls, as though it's the World Series,
a hushed stadium crowded with wig heads,

belt buckles, legless stools, shards of baby food jars.
All marvel at her changeup, her breaking ball, how she
allows nothing, no hits or walks or errors in the field.

The Typists Play Monopoly

Some afternoons I am the thimble.
We are new in this city, lulled
by summer rain and rounding GO
and dice clacking in our loose fists.
My mother rubs the hobo shoe,
her talisman, tells me again
of courteous men in hats
knocking at the back door in 1935,
some missing buttons, laces, teeth.
Eager to accumulate, I take them in,
her stories, pinch my green houses
the size of a thumbnail, groom
my properties—Baltic Avenue,
Mediterranean Avenue, Boardwalk,
Park Place—slums and posh red hotels.
You name it. I'm twelve.
Only ancestors die. Only encyclopedia cities
burn or drown, melt in hot lava.
Without fail, without fanfare,
my mother amasses empires of her own,
acquires the railroads, all four,
a barefoot tycoon in pin curls,
magnanimous, too, with her typewriter,
forgiving pads of paper, a psalm
for my fingers, a chant:
The quick brown fox jumps over the lazy dog.
Again and again, words spool out,
some letters fainter, the *p*, the *a*,
my desire gigantic—speed, precision,
vast neighborhoods on these alluring boards.
I will know bankruptcies over time,
but here, in these wet hours, awash
in five hundreds, goldenrod,
I am the fox, alert, leaping.

Behind the White Bird

after Tatiana Lyskova's painting, White Bird, 2008

Which one of us
holds tighter—you,
timid cockatiel, tall
as a snowman, crown
of green tendrils
curving above our heads?

Or me,
ruby red party dress
spraying past
my hairless thighs
into our kaleidoscope
of a room?

Entranced, claw
to wrist, I give you
a secret name,
whisper into your ear
a charm, a promise
I will break.

One palm
sinks in feathers,
the other, chiffon.
My lips, for now, press
only your white pillow skull.
We do not fly or sing.

May the Road Rise Up

Before she speaks, I hear a faint rumble—wheels
revolving, pedals on this April sidewalk
as I race down apartment stairs, aware
how late I am, how I must strategize
to make up time en route if I'm to get
to church before the Debussy, before

the sermon starts. The girl is 5 (or 4,
perhaps, precociously). Her pink Big Wheel
skids to a halt. She will not let me get
away but commandeers our shared sidewalk
for greeting, poised, polite: "Excuse me," eyes
lock onto mine, all blue, "that sign, BEWARE—"

she points at scrawny, urban tree branch where
discount décor from Halloween hangs for-
lorn, crooked, yet still menacing to eyes
just learning how to read. I sense the wheels
within her mind spin round: *Why warn sidewalk
people? Why scary skulls?* "Did you forget

to take that down?" she queries me to get
assurances the sign belongs elsewhere,
some closet or a drawer, not bright sidewalk,
not April, trees in bloom and, high up, four
wrens singing on a wire. Even the wheels
on the phone poles hum, and I realize

I have not answered yet, am swirling in replies—
what's truest, most like birds? I want to get
this right. She waits, feet planted, sturdy wheels
uncycling, still. "My neighbor keeps BEWARE
on that tree branch. I'm not sure what it's for.
I like how you observe." She nods, sidewalk

a path again for each of us. I walk
to my parked car, she rolls her way, her eyes
continuing to scan. She's looking for
the odd, the beautiful. My prayer? She'll get
new puzzles, dull or shining, everywhere—
schools, temples, forests, mosques, as airplane wheels

touch earth again and taxi to Gate 4.
She'll walk, her bag on wheels, translating signs.
She'll get a cab, meet the driver's eyes, say where.

Ribs

She likes eating with her fingers,
licking tangy barbeque sauce
from thumbtips, grooves
just above nails. She gazes
at people on the sidewalk,
on their way somewhere—
a father wearing his baby
in a pouch, a schoolgirl
humming with answers.

Velocity

Some races end in ties, with victors fused, unclear.
Communal tick of stopwatch second hand. Twinned cheer.
Two breastbones breaking tape.   Two boys on Sunday ran
headlong from curb to street. In my Nissan,
I heard the sluice of denim, braked hard, veered

sharp right. The boys raced left.   I hit a deer
decades ago in West Marin, still hear
the thump and wind in weeds along the median.
Some races end in ties,

burnt rubber, eucalyptus, and a woman near
the corner yelling, *What the fuck!* She slapped car's rear
sloped edge, as though a face, and on the wheel, my hands
ice melting from my wrists.   Would her boys understand
her rage, their names small stones bruising their ears?
Some races end in ties.

Nashville Labyrinth

They're all blue-eyed, these two-year-olds. Some grin
and wave. Some glare, appraising, shrewd. They ride
en masse—red strollers canopied—as I begin

this stone-lined labyrinth, not emptied yet, brochure in-
structing me: *Breathe and clear your mind and step inside*.
They're all blue-eyed, a dozen passengers. Some grin

as though they know already they will win
Grand Prizes. Two or three seem terrified
of crows in seminary cedars. I begin

this maze distracted by a shirt one thin
boy wears: *BAD TO THE BONE*. I'm mystified.
They're all blue-eyed, pre-alphabet. Some grin

and suck their thumbs. We women trade *Mornin'*—
three workers (black), one tourist (white). The workers guide
these heavy strollers past the maze where I begin

my clumsy, walking prayer, my doubts all braided in
a knot, a smaller labyrinth.   *Breathe. Step inside*.
They're all blue-eyed, these two-year-olds. Some grin
and sing a new word: *red, red*.   *Breathe. Begin*.

II. Renters, Vendors, Faux Mountaineers

Renter Sonnet: A Leased Crown

She hangs her yoga pants, petite, across
our shared back porch, one clip for every sock
and bra and thong. So when time comes to toss
foul compost down the shute, I hunch and walk
like Quasimodo through this laundered maze.
It's vexing dodging Calvin Klein prayer flags.
Wait. That's unkind. I'm clueless what she pays
for lingerie. While hunched I don't read tags
en route to shute.   Unneighborly, I know,
this metered airing of minute discord.
Wise souls quit rhyming their complaints and go
ring doorbells, speak aloud needs unignored.
When I at last grow bold, we'll have it out.
By talking trash, we'll make our peace, no doubt.

Renter Sonnet (2)

She's making peace no doubt between the kids
by yelling from the kitchen their first names.
I hear her weariness and clanging lids
and music (not my taste), but no one blames
her for this whirl of sounds. I only wish
for thicker walls, for space between, a yard
of elms. But no, we are conjoined, twin-ish.
We rent identical units. What's hard:
four people live in hers, and two are young
with baby teeth and pup tent beds. The man—
nineteen?—supremely new, invents egg song
they won't forget, then leaves, revs his sedan,
honks a farewell. Inside, she combs their hair
and bickering resumes.   I say a prayer.

Renter Sonnet (3)

I say a prayer for cats dotting windows
and huddling under cars, spooked by this street,
the plump who snooze serene in rooms, and those
whose faces, sizes, names, quirks, and complete
health charts cram flyers tacked to poles.
Rewards are promised, coaxing safe return
of Spanky, Ringo, Cinnamon, Marbles,
asthmatic, microchipped, and shy. Who earns
these prizes? Anyone? Hope withers, wanes
in each apartment on this block. The time
we mourn does vary; some may entertain
their guests of grief for years, no new pets. I'm
inclined to wait, gaze through this glass, revere
the wordless, wild or tame, missing or here.

Renter Sonnet (4)

Come sketch the wordless wild. Climb narrow stairs.
Consider flakes of aqua paint as proof
of passage. Handrail wobbles, creaks. Repairs?
Phone Mr. Tong forthwith, say *fix the roof*,
sing *we are climbing Jacob's ladder*. (No,
scratch that.) Arrive. Angle your face to sky.
Recall your father making his photo.
His art: half clouds, half homes we rent or buy,
all curves and edges, white, gray, black, squares, swirls.
Equation through his lens: the built plus flux
sums up to...what? A sonnet crown? A world?
Stand still. Four floors below cabs, scooters, trucks
and backyard orators blend, blur to mist.
No words but these. They'll stop if you insist.

Renter Sonnet (5)

They stopped. If I, nostalgic, click on DAD,
his e-mails, droll and tender, fill my screen.
Though archive's cobwebbed and dim, I'm glad
I saved a cache, keystroke keepsakes. It's been
five years. I would have liked to write today
and rhapsodize: "I walked in April sun
past Lake Street homes and gardens, past Fung Shui
Supply, Snow White Dry Clean, a new salon—
Face Slapping Spa—and new, chic cat and dog
boutique. The Christian Science Reading Room
moved out. I stood and skimmed the synagogue's
new e-billboard. Dad, every block's in bloom!"
"Must cost a fortune," he'd write back, "to own
a pet, a face, a shirt. E-mail trumps phone."

Renter Sonnet (6)

A face, a shirt, a glowing cigarette—
Alberto, single dad, each night curbside.
He paces, pensive, grim. He may have debt
or trouble with his ex. He doesn't hide
his woes; he sprinkles clues like ashes, small,
combustible. He greets neighbors by rote:
Another day in paradise is all
he says, his irony a dark, thick coat,
no hood or sleeves or warmth. Does it protect
the man? It may, for now. He pulls it tight
and squashes butts beneath his shoe, collects
them, banishing to compost bin, polite.
We share a roof, faucets that drip, and brief
salutes at ten p.m. I smell his grief.

Renter Sonnet (7)

At 10 p.m., eye emptied parking lot.
Praise fog, lone owl. Stow briefcase, Shakespeare. Pile
those earnest midterm essays you have not
read yet. Hear wipers squeaking. Drive.   Meanwhile,
your neighbors exercise, shampoo their hair,
or sing their kids to sleep or rage at God
or scan porn sites et cetera.   Night air
consoles you, most of you, uncertain, flawed,
at home or changing lanes, resolving to
clean litter box, do dreaded laundry in
the morning—sheets, towels, rugs. If nothing's new
under the sun or moon, drive, breathe, begin
to mourn again, dear renter, freshly laundered loss—
a key, wet matches, yoga pants (petite), a cross.

Vacancies

Six hundred signs on window panes, For Lease,
and autumn sun below St. Albert's cross.
This boulevard at dusk, a haunted peace.

All those with wings have hidden, fled—gulls, geese
and ravens, fat from stale pork buns, soy sauce.
Six hundred signs on window panes, For Lease.

Graffitied buses, idling, release
thin plumes of listless passengers, exhaust.
This boulevard at dusk, a haunted peace.

Terse downstairs neighbors hoard apologies
with canned pineapple, bourbon, flashlights, gauze.
Six hundred signs on window panes, For Lease.

These, too, have flown away—our ecstasies,
silk kites. What lingers? Curfews, trespass laws,
this boulevard at dusk, a haunted peace.

Light fades. We fade. No tunes, no melodies,
a limbo in a hush within a pause.
Six hundred signs on window panes, For Lease,
this boulevard at dusk, a haunted peace.

Ticket Stub

I watch the Alexandria decay—
a husk, padlocked ten years, perhaps fifteen,
sadsack NO TRESSPAS signs on entryway
ignored by mice, raccoons. Within, vast screen
once dazzled us before we each acquired
our tiny private slates, before all hell broke loose.
We've spun a kind of hell, each soul now wired
or rather, wireless, linked tight and yet obtuse,
like rusting chains on lonesome theatre.
Why fence an emptiness? Bring wrecking ball,
bring dynamite. Deliver walls from dust, obscure
spray-painted codes. This wordless marquee calls
for mercy, demolition swift and bold,
not limbo, not Eden marooned, unsold.

Breaking Bad Sonnet

I did not sleep till after three last night
replaying scenes from *Breaking Bad*—the taut
finale's bloodied hand of Walter White
descending shiny meth lab vat, gunshot
wound oozing through his shirt, ironic song
accompanying credits one more time.
Awake, I mulled how people's lives go wrong
on HBO and here, these rooms where I'm
supposedly chief author of *my* script.
Right side? No. Left? Tight fetal curl
no sedative, no anodyne, I flipped
like clockwork, walls and ceiling a faint swirl.
Deep night's my meth lab in a pillowed form.
My cushioned head throbs, cooking up a storm.

Shredding

Unglamorous, this chore—
like mowing someone's lawn
without the grass or
sponging plates, no water on.

Pay stubs and cancelled checks,
false starts at villanelles,
suave, stapled sheets—8 max—
grist for this whirring mill.

Save window envelopes.
Why slice? Save pink menus
slid on doorsteps in hopes
we hapless tenants choose

this pizza place, that Thai.
Some documents deserve
no guillotine, hence my
task: sifting to preserve

the useful and the bland,
destroy only numbers,
sleek, vain words from my hand—
supermodel errors.

Why We Have Windows

1 Home

Pinkest of parkas, darkest of
shades, the woman pushing the cart
down the sloped curb of my neighbor's
driveway veils her face, preserves a
privacy as she ferries bag
after bag bursting with cans, thinned
perhaps, by a stomp of her foot,
a quick, bold act punctuating
this winter day in our city,
hers and mine. I can study her
sneakers from here, note their newness,
imagine the sound—shoe sculpting
aluminum. The crack of a
pistol? Whip interrogating
skin? No. This woman, an elder
of our tribe, may bless, thank, each can,
change its shape, send it on its way.

2 Market

Yes, it is vanity that keeps
me here, unfolding frame after
frame of designer eyewear, six
floors up. "Hey! Somebody famous
down there!" A fellow myopic
shopper, delighted, drums on the
thick pane separating us from
winter in the city. I gape,
no, squint, with her at the passing
motorcade, each of us gifted
with temporary spectacles,
imagination, glee. X-ray
vision! "I bet it's the Irish

President," I say. "They move them
around," she says, "they never ride
in the same car." "I bet she's in
that one." I point at the limo
most veiled, most shaded, and we fall
silent, considering the stopped
traffic, the whistling of police,
the ways we keep each other safe.

3 Temple

This day after the rain may be
the best for walking Stow Lake. Few
others are here—a jogger, three
Russian ladies bundled and scarved
from the Avenues, clear plastic
galoshes snapped over their shoes.
I may be looking for something.
Yes, blue herons. Yes, turtles on
thin logs. What breathes beneath the veils
our tribe creates. I find comfort
here, solace in hushed benches
slippery now, their small, wet plaques
honoring past seekers, donors.
And nearing the boathouse, I glimpse
one employee, a teen, unrushed,
no snack bar orders to fill, no
canoes to rent. She stands at a
window, looking out, not at the
lake. She faces another way,
perhaps her future. She looks at
a sprinkling of cars parked in the
lot, beginning slowly to dry.

Many Visitors Have Been Gored

We seek more sky, more falcons circling slow
above us, stiff, screenweary, strapped with gear.
Beware: Do Not Approach the Buffalo,

grim signs, ubiquitous, command—as though
we would, we cautious ones, faux mountaineers
who seek more sky, more falcons circling slow

and fewer thumbtacked edicts, bright yellow
checklists of tasks to do and beasts to fear.
Beware: Do Not Approach the Buffalo.

We hike these trails for balm, touchstones to show
how canyons, geysers, wind outlive us here.
We seek more sky, more falcons circling slow,

observing, tracking all of us below:
Bees, dragonflies, field mice, bobcats, elk, deer,
aware, do not approach the buffalo.

Serenity's elusive, poised to go,
to lunge or gore when predators come near
in search of sky and falcons circling slow.
Beware: Do Not Approach the Buffalo.

At the Marin Art Festival

She spies a vacant tent, vendor AWOL,
and wonders: Kentfield silversmith? Larkspur
soap artisan? Some crisis—thick, not small—
has struck and freed a folding chair for her.
She snags it, grateful for the shade, the view
of Irish fiddlers on the stage engrossed
in jigs from County Donegal and two
blondes, fortysomethings, not quite overdosed
on sound or sun or smack or all of the above,
two whirling dervish babes, their rainbow hula hoops
hypnotic plastic rings symbolic of
some Zen koan perhaps. The Celtic group,
climaxed and coy, agrees to one encore.
Her thoughts ebb—exactly what she came here for.

Bridgework: A Span of Sonnets

The Patrolman's Salutation

You're busted, bub. This keeper of the peace
just clocked your speed at 85, too fast
no matter where, but here—suspended, east-
bound lanes above the bay? Come on, way past
excusable. And I have heard them all:
apologies, threats, alibis, songs, jokes.
Some wink, wave twenties. Others weep, cough, stall.
This job's like bartending—no rum & cokes,
but stories flow behind these steering wheels
as if I laid a napkin down and said,
What will it be? So spare me your appeals,
chit chat, Mr. Lime-Green-Prius-Hybrid-
New Hampshire-plates. Turn your ignition key
to OFF, and you know what to hand to me.

The Toll-Taker's Nightmare

Laid-off. You know, what hands once did replaced
by robots, mute, with gleaming, silver hooks
instead of our cupped palms, long lifelines traced
across our skin. My dream freezes the looks
on drivers' faces craning sunburned necks
at open windows: disbelief and shock
to find machines where people, either sex,
once stood in little booths and played loud rock-
and-roll or gospel on the radio.
Before I wake and slow my racing heart and press
my palm, tender, along my love's pillow,
I see us all sign documents, confess
embezzling each toll. The chief robot
convenes a firing squad. We're hooded, shot.

The Painter's Day Job

Convenient how our squad's jumpsuits have hoods
detachable for days the wind dies down,
for rare, hushed hours, unswaying solitudes.
Most shifts I'm grateful for the layer of cloth around
my ears and jaw. Up here the wind slaps hard
and stings, like nuns when I was nine and drew
werewolves on desks. Yardsticks taught me to guard
my monsters, keep them safe, release only a few
to roam, growl, lunge. *You can't pay the damn bills
by sketching freaks*, my father said. Bridgework, my trade-
off, close enough to coaxing mystery that spills
from fingers onto page or wall or shoulder blade.
We inch along, equipped with canisters of paint,
spray guns, and safety gear—gloves, goggles, clamps, restraint.

The Crisis Counselor's Leave of Absence

A spray of gunfire? No, only staccato gear
of gardeners next door: their lawn mowers
pop, sputter, roar. Still mine, old guilt and fear
if I'm contorting tools, inventing thick showers
of bullets. More appointments with Eileen?
Phone her but brew some coffee first, make toast,
eggs, linger in the tub, put on a clean
shirt. Home, a solace, yes? Believe in ghosts
but only if they're wiser than the dead,
the ones I did not save, talk off the ledge
or catch in mid-air as they fell. The bread
is moldy. When did I last shop? Now hedge-
trimmers begin—a whining, dull lament
for every jump my words could not prevent.

The Driver's Earthquake

for Anamafi Moala Kalushia, 1966-1989

My words could sing. Pretend my words survive
the quake, live past October, promises
to keep or break. Pretend I do not drive
to meet my brother's plane, withhold kisses
instead until he knocks on our front door.
My words could serenade others as well:
the nurses where I work, cashiers in stores,
my husband most of all. Pretend we tell
our children how we met. Pretend they're born.
No, tell the truth. I drove across the bay.
I met his plane. And concrete cracked. They mourn
for me, the kin I left behind. They say
my name, Ana, remember how I spoke
and sang soprano, how a bridge in autumn broke.

The Diplomat's Support Staff

To do in autumn: broker ceasefire, truce.
November ninth we've marked your calendar
to greet the tribes (or are they *sects*? *clans*?) Who's
kidding, let's call these people what they are:
old enemies. Your dance card's full—end
bloodbaths, beget goodwill, release a dove.
We found the dove website, clicked LARGE, pressed SEND.
We booked the Sheraton, reserved a gov-
ernment limo. Your translator's all set
per FBI. We read her file. So please
relax, enjoy your R & R. We have a bet
that San Francisco's cold this month. Felice
lived there and says sometimes the Golden Gate
gets lost in fog. You can't negotiate.

The Traffic Reporter's Retirement Speech

Indulge me. A lost art: you can't steer by my voice,
rush hour duet with helicopter blades,
each freeway snarl, bridge accident relayed with poise,
a muted empathy, plain words. Decades
ago they dubbed me Dawn O'Day. My uniform
a zippered gold lamé jumpsuit, high heels,
headphones. I learned to waltz with thunderstorms
from Steve who flew artillery across rice fields
in Nam. I watched him, stoic, navigate
each element—air, water, earth—to lift
off, circle, land, but could not emulate
my colleague. No, this shifting sky's a gift
to praise, revere. The traffic, too—apologies,
threats, alibis, songs, jokes—a masterpiece.

III. Expiration Dates

Anticipators

for Edsel

Next spring—or sooner—Saturday delivery
will end, reduce to five our days to speak
in passing, you and I, of how our years
speed by and how your shoulder bag grows thin,
hangs lighter now, how you anticipate
new luxuries ahead, pleasure reading

at last, Cervantes, Melville, Proust. No more reading
zip codes through window envelopes, deliveries
of birthday dollars, get well cards, unpaid
gas bills, taxes. In July fog, we speak
with awe of gulls, enormous crows on thin
black wires above the blocks you've walked for years

and we agree: these flocks in recent years
have multiplied, have honed their skills in reading
us and all we carry, all we drop—thin
stuff (transfers, toothpicks, gum)—deliveries
from mouths or pockets straight to gutters, beaks.
No wonder, white and black, they lurk, anticipate

our moves, our scattered crumbs, anticipate
jackpots from Tinkerbell backpacks six-year-
old girls adore.   Dear courier, you speak
of daughters, grown, in cubicles reading
sleek screens, phoning across time zones, delivering
their news—quick bursts of syllables, adieus—and then

silence, for weeks sometimes, perhaps a thin
dribble of lines emailed, attention paid
elsewhere. We nod. We know deliveries

wane, cease as seasons alternate, and years
like crows, fly past. We carry on, reading.
You bring the bundles to my door and speak

of days to come, days full of books that speak
a language almost lost—deep stillness then
deep clarity, a trance only reading
calm hours will weave. We each anticipate
a lightening of load, unhurrying of years,
time ripe for reverence, deliveries

within, unpackaged, vast—special deliveries,
so to speak, birthed by doorstep years reading
and sorting the quotidian, signed, sealed.

Gilbert and Ed Washing the Wheelchairs, Telegraph Avenue Coin-Op

We come each Saturday. Sometimes we sing,
tell knock knock jokes to lighten, lift our chore—
car wash duet, our prayer for bodies aching

in wards of orderlies and moans, in wings
with Ansel Adams prints on walls, Half Dome décor.
We come each Saturday. Sometimes we sing

Sinatra, *fly me to the moon.* We bring
our boom box in the van, open both doors,
          duet, our prayer for bodies aching,

confined to narrow beds, remembering
a picnic, August 1934.
We come each Saturday. Sometimes we sing

but mostly listen to high-powered spray rinsing
these fleets of unfilled seats, each week a dozen more,
          our prayer for bodies aching

we never meet yet surely know, those whispering
our names and words we've heard somewhere before.
We come each Saturday. Sometimes we sing,
                    our bodies aching.

Rented Medicine

So here we sit, alone, outlined with dark,
post-op, film healing underway. No nar-
cotics in pills compete, no soup or cat
who dozes, purrs near small incisions that
the surgeon drew. I drove across the park

last week, fed meter, climbed steep stairs—no lark,
no whim—laid hands on classics: comic arc,
brisk repartee, fox furs and silk cravats.
So here we sit.

They buoy me: Marilyn, Tony and Jack
onboard a train. Woody's trenchant sad sack.
Beloved mobsters, bellboys, diplomats
parade through time—loyal, immediate
balm in the dark. Next week I take them back.
So here we sit.

January in Gualala

what does she desire most

mastering arts
solace within endings
seeds within ruins

another ripe kiwi
another shaft of sun
in old, wet forest
where living and dying
need no announcement

A Broken World: Cento for Jane Clarke

Lifting our words like debris
we talk about the land, the ditches,
but before the breakfast tea is cold
promise to carry each other
when the days are short of light,
like days of Wicklow rain.

I think of the herd of cows,
lights coming on in the house, how we longed
when we talked of lost villages, lost streets.
Do you remember the bell across the river,
smooth and slow past stands of alder?
We'd slip the catch on the rusted chain.

A crack, a hush, a broken world rolls
as if it belonged to someone else—
she's forgotten your name, sees her sister in your face
or the one who pulls ragwort on her knees.
I opened the cage of my fingers
though I don't know why. Is it the swallow's nest?

Let there be wind
and a song thrown to the sky,
stories for people who worked the soil
speckled with yellow iris, bordered with sedge.
I can't promise it's flawless as honey
or meadow-grass heavy with dew.

The Elder

Merlin is 13 years, 10 months old…He is to become the oldest raccoon ever on record in California and will break the record for the current oldest raccoon in North America.
—San Francisco *Chronicle*, February 21, 2014

He sleeps through nights, his prowling over. Wild,
the others seize the dark, die young, by three.
Hunched, hardly masked, Merlin has us beguiled.
How has he weathered his captivity
since losing Lance, his brother, long ago,
since losing any chance to steal away?
His keeper holds him close in this photo
and rubs his bony spine as if to say
You do belong with us. She feeds him grapes,
mice, trout puréed, and maybe Merlin purrs,
a ragged hum, resigned to life with no escapes,
no redwood groves, no toppling garbage cans, neighbors
disturbed from dreams of thieves. Do human hands console,
relieve his aches, return enough of all we stole?

This One

In a Hunan restaurant
the night we became lovers
a family next to us
sent back the food
    This is way too hot

You rubbed my hands
cold from our lingering
on the Filbert stairs
asked about my rings

Birthstone
Thailand
grandfather polishing
turquoise in his garage

And this one
oval of onyx
mother-of-pearl
carnelian
a longer answer

The most erotic thing
a man can do in public
is listen to a woman
telling a story

Clutter Song

He's traced to cat fur, dust, his allergies
and pats down pockets daily: glasses, phone.
His crowded sink—bowls, mugs—cries out *A squeeze
of lemon Joy! A sponge!* Yes, I have grown
accustomed to his habits, to his lair,
as he, to mine: low mumbling in my sleep,
the ceiling mold, the drainpipes clogged with hair,
my stacks, unread. What curse to cling, to keep
so much, so long, past expiration dates,
past reason, rhyme! My love—wise soul—forgives
this hoarding, builds his crooked towers too, creates
sculptures of envelopes, all he receives:
appeals from orphans, monks, Greenpeace campaigns.
Concerned, but broke—like me—he saves, and he refrains.

Phone Call in a New Century: Cento
for Lynne Barnes

Right here under my roof
the word *utopia* raises last wild hopes.
We tried to think of everything.
The times were swelling with whitecaps of change.
We had long halcyon periods
as we caught lightning bugs and dropped them into jars.
Towards the end, sometimes they opened.

The telephone rings and its blue flame leaps
like an unmoored kite,
a frightened lizard
on the grounds of an old indigo plantation.
In a fireproof beekeeper's suit,
I swallow the night
like a cavern on a windswept mountain.

Here comes the future
sneaking outside to the backyard for a smoke,
running in the warm air along the deer traces
and I grasp it with both hands, pull my life,
and try to tell you
emerald needles of thriving seedlings now touch,
the hawthorn carries a faint fragrance of sea.

Sestina in Late June

My summer quest: to be a graceful guest,
to mind my P's and Q's, unrumple beds,
nix shouting in my sleep, take heed to close
each toilet lid (or not), befriend small birds
that serenade at dawn from stiff phone lines
in neighborhoods of in-laws young and old.

I'm stiff myself this year, not limber, old
knots of worry in my shoulders, not guests
but residents. My face at fifty: lines
and leaky eyes, chin hairs. A queen-size bed
now *de rigueur*. No eating like a bird
for me! I prize my appetite. (My clothes,

no mystery, feel snug. Zippers don't close
the way they slid in 1990. Old
blue jeans, size 12: bargains for early birds
combing yard sales.) A ruminating guest
in Philadelphia, I hope this bed
has no denomination, no hard line

stance, simply cedar. Should I toe some line?
This *is* a Catholic home, and I lie close
to Tom, both naked in his sister Brenda's bed
just borrowed for our stay. So many old
beliefs bedevil me. Which ones are mine, Ms. Guest-
from-California? I consider birds.

Vic, Brenda's husband, wakes to feed wild birds
at 6 a.m. He worked assembly line,
Nabisco, fifty years, he growls at guests.
All them cookies. Blue jays, finches crowd close,
evaluate his slippers, crumbs—stale, old.
Vic folds and stacks our laundry neatly on the bed,

and adds a faded snapshot—cat, long gone—embeds
a caption, shaky script: *my baby.*   Birds,
Tom, Brenda, Vic, and I—we all grow old.
We give and take and give. They shift, these lines.
They swirl, all these beliefs we carry close—
not pets, not Smokey, Sunburst—more like guests

invited for a while, or hungry birds. We're close
and then we scatter, flee to branches, power lines.
We're guests, awake or sleeping in old beds.

For the Man at Macy's Lurking in Swimwear

Don't think I didn't notice you. I did.
But that's your fervent hope, to creep us out,
we fiftysomethings on our lunch breaks, mid-
April, determination mixed with doubt.
Our quest: acquire a bargain, flattering,
dark, dignified, a hint of whimsy though,
a Helen Mirren suit for traveling
to hotel pools, a beach in Mexico.
But you, sir, crouching by the clearance rack,
were in the way, a cone some road crew left behind.
I steered around, bypassed you, but looked back
and saw a loneliness I sometimes find
in mirrors as I brush my teeth or drive.
Awash in teal, the two of us, alone, alive.

Souvenir Corkscrew

These words rub off, bleed faintly in her hand
with every twist, a hundred every week.
Old tour—a mute ghost ship, mirage island

that beckons, winks on a horizon, and
then vanishes. Once scarlet cursive, sleek,
fine words rub off, bleed faintly in her hand.

Each glass she pours, the less she understands
of history, the more she rusts, a plump antique.
Her tour—a mute ghost ship, mirage island.

July blind date in another century? A grand
adventure, honeymoon? Perhaps. Now weak,
more words rub off, bleed faintly in her hand,

a taunting cabernet. She never planned
to shatter soapy goblets, slice wet palms, flinch, shriek.
Old tour—a mute ghost ship, mirage island

each night at table, sink, and bed. How to withstand
slow liquid loss of memory? Just speak:
All words rub off, bleed faintly in her hand.
Her tour—a mute ghost ship, mirage island.

IV. Lighter Than Her Lace: A Crown of Borrowed Self-Portraits

Lighter Than Her Lace: A Crown of Borrowed Self-Portraits

Sofonisba Anguissola, *Self-Portrait at the Clavichord,* 1561

Her choice: Depict two women's faces, old
in shadow, young in light with fingertips
arranged expert on keys, as she will hold
her brushes in the Spanish court, paint lips
and eyes and gowns of Isabella, queen
and confidante. The painter-sitter here—
a knowing gaze, white lace collar, serene
and chaperoned by age, common, austere,
a witness to the making, neither muse
nor menace. Woman, elder, half in dark,
we do not see your hands. Perhaps you use
them for creating too. You leave your mark
off-canvas, yet within. This song of self unites
crone, gifted girl, a clavichord's keys, blacks and whites.

Clara Peeters, *Vanitas Self-Portrait*, c. 1610

No clavichord. The only black and white
a pair of dice, a five and three faced out
to viewers of her self with gilt still-life,
bouquet in bloom, save one, listless petals about
to drop among the coins, the gems, fine tray
tipped, toppled, not upright. And she, in pearls
at throat, both wrists, red hair, shuns, turns away
from opulence that's half her crafted world,
beguiling then and now, ensnaring us
in borrowing or gambling debt. Her dice
no accident, no fluke. But what purpose
this bubble she pretends eludes her eyes?
Orb, drifting, sheerer, lighter than her lace.
Her fleeting globe—and ours—time will erase.

Angelica Kauffman, *Self-Portrait Hesitating Between the Arts of Music and Painting, 1791*

Time will erase her quandary. Now she prays,
dreams, seeks the counsel of a priest who hears
dilemmas every day. He pauses, says,
My child, your songs do echo in God's ears
and yet your palette gives enduring praise.
The climb toward God is steep, uneven, long.
While journeying, clasp hands with Art always.
And so she does.   In Rome, at 50, strong,
and wife to Zucchi, fellow painter, she
returns to ache of youth, unknowing place:
　　A red-gowned Music tugs one hand tightly,
　　fresh garlands on her brow, sweet yearning face,
　　while Painting, urgent, right arm free, points up a hill.
　　Angelica, in white, between the two, stands still.

Edouard Louis Dubufe, *Portrait of Rosa Bonheur*, 1857

We two stand still—absurd!—yet I prefer
this pair to his first sketch: Bonheur idle
at oak table. Cliché! Inferior,
mon dieu, to my new pose: Bonheur with bull.
No one disputes my genius bringing beasts
alive by brushstroke, rendering each mane,
each hoof, horn, nostril, burr—deft expertise.
Still, inquiry demands disguise. I feign
a manly stride in trousers, cravat, cloak
to venture out to slaughterhouse, pierce through
banalities—limp, ladylike—peel back
smooth surfaces to animal sinew.
His table, I replace, of course. Instead,
my legacy: male creature's muscled head.

Laura Knight, *Self-Portrait*, 1913

How holy is the human body when bare of other than the sun.
                    —Laura Knight, *The Magic of a Line,* 1965

My legacy? Hmm. My sketchbooks—penciled nudes—
will not survive the Cornwall damp. Each page
will gum and stink of mildew. Platitudes,
as well, will curdle for some years: *Outrage!*
Indecent! How dare she? Yet I must dare
to paint my self, hair tucked inside black hat,
my face in profile, gazing at her bare
and holy body—Ella, friend, palms at
her skull, feet steady on striped cloth, her spine
unclothed, unbent. My model will not live
as long as I. She will not praise light nine
decades, mourn two world wars. But we will give
beyond this red of sweater, cream and pink
of skin. What lasts? Discovering, I think.

Alice Neel, *Nude Self-Portrait*, 1980

Dear Alice, kin, what lasts? Your daughters die.
Firstborn, diphtheria, the second, suicide.
One lover slashes fifty canvases, and I
admit even this sonnet strays, threatens to hide
in idly Googling sites that document
desertions, opium, shoplifting food.
Bouquets, but questions for you, Alice, shoulders bent
at 80, glasses crooked, Mother Hubbard nude
on blue striped chair, your irises this shade
of azure too. I cheer your nakedness
and try to read your face. Have you conveyed
some wisdom of the very old? Or wariness
may simply be your signature. Each face
you paint—not quite alarmed, just shy of grace.

Carol Greene, *Self-Portrait*, 2009

You paint not troubled souls but harmony:
Calm, bare-armed girl, first flute. Gray-goateed man
in white shirt, humming, burps a grandbaby.
You smile in aqua turtleneck. I can
imagine how you tucked your photograph
beside this canvas, looked long, listened, chose
a slender brush, embarked on song of self:
One shadowed cheek, one bright. Peach hues for nose.
Reflected glints in oval lenses. Eyes—
like Alice's, like mine—the useful blue
of ocean, sky, and wing that shimmer, rise,
and blur beyond your studio, same blue
as backdrop cradling white crown, each wrinkle, fold
of flesh. New, lilting hymn to women's faces, old.

Notes

"Considering Chess, Tomales Bay"
George Koltanowski (1903-2000) was a Belgian American chess player, promoter, and writer. For over fifty years, "Kolty" wrote a daily chess column for the San Francisco *Chronicle*.

"Breaking Bad Sonnet"
Vince Gilligan created and produced the 2008-2013 television series "Breaking Bad." Bryan Cranston plays Walter White, a high school chemistry teacher diagnosed with inoperable cancer who makes and sells crystallized methamphetamine to ensure financial security for his family.

"Many Visitors Have Been Gored"
The poem's title is lifted directly from flyers in parking lots of Yellowstone National Park.

"The Driver's Earthquake"
Anamafi Moala Kalushia died from injuries on the Bay Bridge in the aftermath of the Loma Prieta earthquake in northern California on October 17, 1989.

"The Traffic Reporter's Retirement Speech"
Kelly Lange (born Dorothy Scafard in 1937) was the first woman hired to report on Los Angeles morning traffic from helicopters in the 1960s. She worked for radio station KABC-AM 790 and used the name "Dawn O'Day."

"Rented Medicine"
The first line is borrowed from Kim Bridgford's sonnet, "Hollywood," from her collection, *Hitchcock's Coffin: Sonnets about Classic Films* (David Robert Books, 2011).

"A Broken World: Cento for Jane Clarke"
Jane Clarke grew up on a farm in the west of Ireland. Her poems appear widely in Ireland and the U.S., and she won the Listowel Writers' Week Poetry Collection Prize in 2014 for *The River* (Bloodaxe Books).

"The Elder"
The epigraph is from a February 21, 2014 San Francisco *Chronicle* article, "New Roomies for Oldest Raccoon in Captivity."

"Phone Call in a New Century: Cento for Lynne Barnes"
Born in Georgia in 1946, Lynne Barnes lived in a Haight Ashbury commune in San Francisco from 1972-1992. The cento honors her poetry collection, *Falling Into Flowers* (Blue Light Press, 2017), a nuanced self-portrait, tender and powerful.

"For the Man at Macy's Lurking in Swimwear"
Helen Mirren is an award-winning English actress. Her career began in the Royal Shakespeare Company in the late 1960s and includes work in film, television, and theater.

"Lighter Than Her Lace: A Crown of Borrowed Self Portraits"
The inspiration for this sequence is Frances Borzello's richly illustrated book, *Seeing Ourselves: Women's Self-Portraits* (Harry N. Abrams, Inc. Publishers, 1998).

"Edouard Louis Dubufe, *Portrait of Rosa Bonheur*, 1857"
Though not a self-portrait *per se*, this work includes a bull painted by Rosa Bonheur, a celebrated animal painter. Bonheur often dressed as a man in public.

"Laura Knight, *Self-Portrait*, 1913"
The epigraph is from Laura Knight's autobiography, *The Magic of a Line* (William Kimber and Co., 1965).

"Carol Greene, *Self-Portrait*, 2009"
For many years Carol Greene lived and painted in San Jose, California, the city of my birth.

About the Author

Kathleen McClung, a native of northern California, is the author of the 2013 chapbook *Almost the Rowboat*. Her work appears widely in journals and anthologies including *Atlanta Review, Ekphrasis, Mezzo Cammin, The MacGuffin, Peacock Journal, Unsplendid, Raising Lilly Ledbetter: Women Poets Occupy the Work Space*, and *A Bird Black as the Sun: California Poets on Crows and Ravens*.

Winner of the Rita Dove and Maria W. Faust poetry prizes, she was the winner of the inaugural Shirley McClure poetry prize at the 2016 Los Gatos Listowel Writers' Festival and winner of the grand prize of the Ina Coolbrith Circle 2017 poetry contest. McClung is a three-time finalist for the Morton Marr poetry prize and a Pushcart and Best of the Net nominee. She serves as associate director of the Soul-Making Keats literary competition and sponsor/judge of the sonnet category, and she presents at readings, panels and workshops across the country.

She holds masters degrees in education and English from Stanford University and California State University Fresno and teaches at Skyline College and The Writing Salon. She directs Women on Writing: WOW! Voices Now on the Skyline campus, celebrating creativity in writers of all ages. She lives in San Francisco.

www.ingramcontent.com/pod-product-compliance
Lightning Source LLC
Chambersburg PA
CBHW071109090426
42737CB00013B/2548